AN ENTREPRENEUR'S STORY OF PERSISTENCE

# No Secrets to Elevation

CALVIN MILLS, JR.

NO SECRETS TO ELEVATION:
AN ENTREPRENEUR'S STORY OF PERSISTENCE

Copyright © 2018 Calvin Mills, Jr.

ISBN-13: 978-1986911368
ISBN-10: 1986911365

*I dedicate this book to anyone who has had a door slammed in their face and to anyone who has been told it's impossible for them to achieve their dreams. My story is proof that you can do whatever you set your mind to accomplish.*

*I also dedicate this book to my mom, my beautiful wife, Brittany, my children, my brothers, and other family and friends who have stuck by me through it all. I love all of you.*

# CONTENTS

Whenever you see a successful person, you only see the public glories, never the private sacrifices and obstacles it took to reach that success.

Cherish your
visions and your dreams
as they are the children
of your soul,
the blueprints of your
achievements.

# *Foreword*

When I first heard the name Calvin Mills Jr., two esteemed men, Rolfe McCollister, the Founder and CEO of Louisiana Business Inc., and George Bevan, an executive of Shaw Group Inc., were on the other end of the phone asking me to meet a nice young man who was trying to start a business.

They knew I was the right person for Calvin to meet. As the Executive Director and Founder of Louisiana State University (LSU) Innovation Park and Louisiana Business Technology Center, I was responsible for the economic development mission of LSU and for assisting small business owners, entrepreneurs and innovators achieve their dreams by starting successful businesses.

The next day, entering the room was this "mountain of a man" named Calvin Mills. I talked with him, as I do with most entrepreneurs seeking help. We took the time to learn about each other, and we thoroughly discussed his business idea. Toward the end of our meeting, I gave him a list of people to see, assignments to work on, and things to read and research before coming back for a second meeting. This generally takes most entrepreneurs a month to complete, *if ever*.

But not Calvin.

He was back in my office four days later asking, "What's next?"

Let me tell you, I was shocked and impressed. At this point, I knew that Calvin would be successful. We scheduled times to meet over the course of the next two months, and each time, he produced the same, speedy results. I could tell that he was serious about his vision, business and drive for success. I saw myself in him.

As someone who has had many successes but also many setbacks, I've always taken an approach that stems from one fact: *my future is up to me*. I come from a first-generation Italian immigrant family whose father worked two jobs. From watching him, I learned that you have to work for what you get and you have to do what it takes to be successful and support those counting on you. I was fortunate to have parents that instilled a strong work ethic and sense of family into my siblings and me.

My drive eventually led me to go after a college education, even though my parents had barely achieved a high school level of education. I later worked for NASA in a space program, and from there, I went on to own and operate 10 businesses — all leading to a spearheading career and mission with entrepreneurs today.

Calvin made my job of being his business counselor and mentor easy. In no time, he launched his business, and that day, I told him what I tell all of our clients at LSU Innovation Park. *You are a client for life.*

After 15 years, that statement proves to be true. Calvin continues to exercise his right to call for advice whenever he feels he needs a second opinion or someone to verify his thoughts and ideas. We meet regularly to tweak his business plan and make adjustments whenever a situation requires him to do so. (*Business plans are not static. They are working documents that must be adjusted and corrected on a regular basis.*) He even drops in or calls when things are not going well and he needs a boost or when things are going great and he needs a reality check. (*We all need that sometimes!*)

Growing beyond mentorship, I feel that my relationship with Calvin has shifted into one that makes him more of a protégé than a mentee and a resource I refer to others for guidance.

I certainly am proud of him and all that he has accomplished. He did not have the background and breaks that many successful entrepreneurs start with. He learned from his up-bringing to take responsibility for his success and make things happen. I admire him for that and for the example he continues to set for others coming from similar backgrounds and environments. I am a fan of his, and I am convinced that he is one of the most suited men to convey such an inspiring, awakening and real message about the process of elevating in entrepreneurship.

Why am I a bona fide believer of his ability to make a difference? Well, one of my favorite examples of why can be traced back to a day in 2006 when I asked him to speak to a group of disadvantaged students who were visiting the LSU Innovation Park for a tour and field day.

Calvin began his message by telling them how he became a successful entrepreneur in the Information Technology (IT) Sector. A disinterested young man in the back was slouched in his desk, not listening and disrupting others. Calvin asked him if he had a question. The young man jokingly replied, "Yeah. How many touchdowns did you score in the NFL?" Calvin didn't miss a beat when he responded, "Sit up straight and listen to what I'm saying. Football allowed me to get a college education, and the NFL got me two bad knees and the seed money that I needed to start my company. I am here today to tell you that my success is based on my college education, hard work, and discipline — not running with a football."

I was moved by that statement and so was the entire class of students. That kid in the back suddenly began to pay attention. If I delivered that message, it would not have gotten the same impact. The fact that the message came from Calvin made the difference. A tall, athletic-built, impressive player and individual who intensely states that it was his brain and not his muscles that made him successful is a powerful message to disadvantaged kids — no, to *all* kids.

Calvin is fearless, and I don't mean on the football field. He is not afraid of trying new things and of failing. All successful entrepreneurs have failed. I think Calvin realized early on that he had to take control of his life and escape from the environment that dooms many minority youth.

He used his athletic skills to get what he needed — an education, network, and self-confidence. He maneuvered that into starting a successful business and learning IT skills at an early age. At some point, he even had two jobs and did outside IT services just to pay off debts. He did what he had to do to get himself on a sound financial basis. While doing this, he met Rolfe McCollister, George Bevan, and many more people who believed in him and assisted him in his move forward. He never felt sorry for himself or made excuses. He made his success one day at a time.

Nothing has been handed to Calvin Mills. He earned every bit of it. He earned the trust of everyone in his network by doing right. In *No Secrets to Elevation*, you will understand that there are no shortcuts or easy ways to success, but Calvin's story, wisdom, and knowledge will be a keepsake of influence for you to continue going and growing throughout your career and life.

**By: Charles F. D'Agostino, MBA**
*Founder of LSU Innovation Park &*
*Louisiana Business & Technology Center*

The question is not,
"What does it cost?"
The question is how
much are you willing to
invest mentally,
emotionally and
physically to turn your
vision into reality?

If you are willing to do only what's easy, life will be hard. But, if you are willing to do what's hard, life will be easy.

# Introduction

"What's the secret to — ?" many begin to ask, eager to get their new ideas off the ground.

"There is no secret," I quickly cut in without pausing to think twice. My answer is always the same. We are as successful as we want to be.

If I was asked to define entrepreneurship, I would do it in one word: *persistence*. I believe success hangs on the very principle of persistence — "to remain unchanged in a character, condition or position." That's a path to success, plain and simple. It means to remain fixed on the dream, in character, condition and position, regardless of anything trying to pull you away from it.

This type of endurance sums up the story of my life and my journey to continuous growth and success. I've learned that regardless of working the popular strategies that everyone says "work," there has to be persistence in the picture. Without it, there will be no consistent elevation in your life or business.

Here's what most people who want to be an entrepreneur will do. They will come up with a good idea, possibly create that idea, and then give up or reason with not going any further with what they've created. Why is that? Because, most are not truly motivated to keep moving or building through to the next steps. Deep down they don't *really* believe it can be done — or worse, they don't want to wait for it to grow. As a result, their persistence suffers through the process.

If you want to successfully carry out a vision with steady elevation, you have to consistently say it, desire it, believe in it and move toward it. When you truly believe in your vision, you'll act in a way that supports it for the long haul.

Again, we are as successful as we want to be. The answer to elevation is always right in front of you. When you wake up in the morning and look in the mirror, you'll be staring at the answer.

*You* are the secret.

You'll be the secret today, tomorrow and forever, so don't waste time ignoring what's already inside of you; use what you have to your advantage.

Challenges are what make life interesting and overcoming them is what makes life meaningful. Never fear failing at something because there's something you have to learn.

Age is a measurement used to identify how long you've been alive. It doesn't gauge your maturity, common sense, ability to handle situations, or anything else.

# 1

## *Vision in a Dark Beginning*

I UNDERSTOOD THE MEANING OF strength at a young age. The kind of strength they don't tell you about in school The kind you can only experience through ruthless surroundings that are constantly forcing you to either survive it or become it.

No stranger to that type of pressure growing up, I can say I chose to survive it. A few blocks down from the Calliope Projects in New Orleans, Louisiana, I survived the Third Ward.

With one parent, I survived.

My father hadn't been around since I was three years old. Not because he was a deadbeat, but because he didn't survive the seven gunshots to his back one afternoon. Six months after he was hit, he took his last breath lying on a hos-pital bed.

Watching people shoot each other and sometimes die right in the middle of the street was nothing out of the ordinary. Nor was stealing, getting arrested, using drugs, selling drugs or anything like that considered out of the ordinary to see. It happened every day, on every corner. So, yes, from the steps of my house, I saw things that a child my age should've never seen or have ever been forced to survive.

However, inside of my home, I saw a different story. A story I could focus on becoming.

Behind the ragged closed doors of a two-bedroom shotgun house with no central air and many times no running water, I saw a woman studying for college courses, working multiple jobs, dropping everything to volunteer for others and sacrificing all she had to ensure that my education and childhood experiences weren't limited. She was (and *still* is), by far, my greatest example of persistence and sacrifice.

Living without my father was tough for both of us, but my mom never once stopped going after her dreams. She stayed focused on both of our destinies. The day she received her college degree and walked across the stage of Southern University, with my hand gripped inside of hers, I witnessed the meaning of strength for the first time. It meant to survive unfortunate surroundings. It meant to grab ahold of the bright vision ahead despite any dark beginnings in your way.

My mother is the strongest person I know. Even when things were obviously hard for us back then, she didn't show it. I *knew* we were poor (considering my cold feet and painful stomach aches), but many of my childhood experiences were that of a rich kid. My extended family members had even nicknamed me *the little poor rich kid*, because in the midst of my mom scraping pennies to pay the bills, she found an inexpensive way to expose me to different cultures and opportunities.

For instance, I played golf, but I only went to the free golf classes. I played tennis, but I only went to the free tennis classes. I played soccer, basketball and football for the school. I played the violin, but it was a friend of the family who gave me the violin. I played the saxophone, but a famous, family friend who gave me the saxophone and agreed to teach me how to play. I was enrolled in De La Salle High, a private Catholic school, and the tuition was totally out of our budget. Yet, my schooling was afforded through a work-study program that granted us a reduced tuition fee.

So, you see, I wasn't "lucky" with nice things, but I was blessed to have the strength of my mom, a dreamer right in front of me, who always found a way out of no way.

Sometimes not settling for harsh or unfavorable surroundings means taking a minute to look around and see where you can find the light. My light was shining through my mother.

I had my heart and mind set on improving our lives for the future. I also saw light in my god-father who'd stepped up to the plate as both a father-figure and a role model when my dad died. Your light is somewhere around you too. It can be a teacher, a friend, a friend's parent, a neighbor, a family member, or even a dream burning in your gut. Regardless of where it comes from, the day you see it and are inspired by it is the day you stop settling for your sur-roundings.

***

"You're a sell out!" That's what I'd hear neighborhood kids yelling as I walked past them on my way to school. They didn't know the sacrifices my mom and I were making to keep me in private school. All they knew was that I hung around white people all day — which I can agree made me a bit "different."

There were only a handful of black students

at the school, so walking through the doors was like walking into a completely different world every day. In the mornings, I'd stroll three blocks from my street to the Napoleon bus stop, and before I knew it, I'd be transferred into the world of the rich, passing beautiful homes and big yards. In the evenings, when my classmates were going back to their nice homes, I was being dropped back off to my poor neighborhood.

To no surprise, I was the kid who the girls didn't like and the boys wanted to bully — both at school and on our street. I was the one without a new bike on Christmas day, wearing Payless shoes and hand-me-down clothes, with a Nintendo on layaway for a year and one school uniform in my closet. Some days, I'd run home from school afraid to fight. They'd especially tease the way I was dressed and try to intimidate me.

Did I spend time crying? Yes. Was I sad about my situation? Of course.

There were countless moments of feeling disappointed and embarrassed, but I always saw something better for myself. I didn't settle for my surroundings. Like my mom, I knew if I wanted a bright future, I had to stay focused.

Like I said, I was riding the reduced rate of the school's work-study program. If you don't know what it means to do work-study, I'll paint you a picture. It means that during lunchtime, you're the kid serving lunch before sitting down to eat. It means that after running touchdowns on the football field on a Friday night, you're waking up early Saturday morning to cut grass at the school. It means that you even spend your summers cleaning all sorts of areas on the school's campus.

Work-study didn't feel *or* look cool — ever! But, inevitably, the responsibilities it brought on pushed me to mature faster. While my mom was working, sometimes two jobs, to make sure my future and the bills were paid on time, I wasn't far behind her, giving up weekends and afternoons for work-study duties. As far as I was concerned, I was the man of the house. I focused on taking care of whatever she needed and made the necessary sacrifices to help support her.

What I didn't know then but I know now is that a main key to elevation is sacrifice. If you want to become successful or legendary, first understand what it means to make some sacrifices. A major problem with our society today is that we want everything "now," and this keeps us from putting in the work needed to achieve the things we dream of. Regardless of where you want to end up, sacrifice is where it starts.

Now, here's what I learned to be just as important as sacrifice: the people you surround yourself with.

The surroundings you *can* control are worth your attention. You can't afford to allow negative people or negative conversations get in the way of your growth. I had to learn this lesson early on in life. Wanting more for myself meant that I couldn't hang around the guys on my street too often. I knew being in their company and a part of their conversations would lead me down a path I wasn't interested in following.

## Sacrifice:

*In order to be successful, you must first know your path and then be ready to walk it.*

Going down any path to success also means having to endure certain sacrifices that come along with the circumstances on that route. First, it's important not to overthink the path. Everyone's path to the same end result of "success" can be totally different.

Let's say you and a friend both want to be a successful entrepreneur selling snowballs. Your friend may want to find an investor first. You may say you're investing your own money.

Just like a roadmap to any location, there are hundreds of different paths you can take to reach the same destination. Paths to success are unique, but regardless of the one you take, be ready to make whatever sacrifice it requires.

Your life does not get
better by chance.
It gets better by *change.*

Genius is the ability to put into effect what is in your mind.

# 2

## *An Entrepreneur's Mindset*

T HERE WERE TWO guys that I related to most at school — Damion and Kenneth. We came from similar backgrounds. A lot like my situation, their mom was a single parent who worked twice as hard to give her children as many opportunities as she could. With friends like Damion and Kenneth who, like me, wanted more for themselves, I was able to talk about everything I wanted to accomplish when I got older.

Both Damion and Kenneth were extremely smart — top of their classes and rock stars in my eyes. Kenneth, the oldest of us three, graduated valedictorian. And if I'm being completely honest, he was such a cool, laid-back guy that it was hard not to want to be like him.

Me? I was the athlete of our crew. They were the brains. I didn't make straight A's or get the special smart-kid recognition, but Damion and Kenneth did! That says a lot about how I felt about myself. I hung around them because that was the direction I wanted to go in. On a regular basis, they reminded me to consider my future and not sell myself short academically.

Kenneth would say things like, "Cal, make sure you keep your grades up so you can get a scholarship for football." It encouraged me to keep going after the best opportunities in front of me. Kenneth didn't know it at the time, but although he was only a year older than me, he was one of my biggest inspirations.

Conversations with both of them sparked motivation in me, and they still do today. As I stated before, the surroundings you can control are worth your attention. Hang around those who are drawing out your greatest potential and talking with you about your growth. Ask yourself, "What are my friends saying about my life?" Are they talking about elevation or discussing the decline of others? If it's not about elevation, it's not worth your time.

Another good question I'd like to ask here is, "What are you saying to yourself?" Growing up, I told myself I wouldn't live in poverty ever again. So, I didn't allow thoughts of not having enough consume me. Instead, I let it motivate me to push harder. I knew that if I could make it out of my situation, I could do for my mom what she had done for me. For a long time, I told myself that football would be the thing to deliver the lavish lifestyle I saw for myself and my mom.

I was wrong.

I learned that a career as a professional football player wasn't all that it was cracked up to be.

First, you should know that my football skills didn't come about organically and pursuing the sport professionally was a BIG dream that I had to work excessively hard at reaching. For instance, when I initially joined the high school team, I struggled to find my place. But, over time, I became a force to be reckoned with on the field. I gained so much respect that by my senior year, they named me the captain of the team.

However, when it was time for college and trying out for the team at Southern University, the coach told me I was wasting my time. Not walking away, I used my salesman-like mouthpiece to talk my way on the team that year, and soon after, I became a player that the coach admitted he would've been sorry to pass up on. I had to put in hard work to prove myself and fight for what I wanted. While I was there, we became three-time champions.

Having success on the field and taking college courses didn't change the fact that my mind was wired to think like an entrepreneur. I approached school as if it was a business. It wasn't playtime for me. I took it so serious that I wore suits to all of my classes. (*Yes, suits!*) My appearance brought on a lot of attention and a lot of unnecessary jokes from other students.

My freshman year was tough. I had moments where I felt like people didn't like me for no reason. And the entire time, I was trying to be a good student, teammate and to get along with everyone.

The good news is that I didn't do it to prove anything to anyone; I did it for myself. So, when they picked on me, I didn't drown in the bad energy. I channeled it to win both on and off the field.

I was studying programming as a computer science major. My love for the information technology world had started early. I would ponder on the things I wanted to do after going pro and think of ways to excel beyond getting a job as a programmer. My underlining desire was to own a business one day.

I believe, we all yearn to have something of our own one day. I often say that we are all born with an entrepreneurial spirit. But here's the thing: when we become a part of the school system, that spirit is usually lost. Schools aren't internally structured to teach us how to be entrepreneurs. They teach us how to get a good education, a secure job and then retire.

I'm not built that way.

I don't believe you are either.

We want to be in control of our destinies, right? We want to create and produce, not only consume and do as we are told. We're not robots. We want to live out our dreams, not our duties. We want a long-term plan that still includes endless, unexpected opportunities.

\*\*\*

My entrepreneurial mindset turned out to be the perfect attribute after trying out for an NFL team. When I got to the evaluation camp, it was nothing like I imagined. I quickly learned that the process was fast, and if you weren't a high-draft pick, it wasn't what you thought it would be. I saw grown men crying and quitting every other day, and I knew this wasn't what I wanted for my life.

My thoughts of the NFL being a golden opportunity in life and my chance to be rich enough to take care of my mom changed. I didn't look at this so-called dream the same anymore, especially since it didn't compare to the satisfaction of starting my own company. I left and never looked back.

When I returned to college, I knew two things for sure: I loved helping people and I wanted to work in the community hands-on. I decided to take what I understood about my gifts and go after what I was purposed to do.

Years of watching my mom's smile pierce through our darkest moments gave me hope and a sense of confidence in what was possible. It led me to believe that things can *always* get better. Now, when I see something I want in life, I go after it. I seek and find out how to make it come to life, regardless of adversities along the way.

My mom found the best in every bad situation. She didn't just accept it for what it was. She grew forward from it. And that's the type of person I've become — someone who moves forward and continues to have vision in their darkest times.

# Character:

*You cannot be what you're not, but you can become what you're not.*

You can't say you're an athlete without putting in the work to be an athlete. You can't say you're an athlete and you don't play any sports.

You can't be something you haven't actively been doing. This goes for your character as well. For example, you may say you're a quiet person and not a "people person." But you can't be a people person if you don't open up to being more friendly and outgoing around people. Just because you're not a people person today doesn't mean you can't become a people a person over time. Character is developed!

The more you practice and build a certain characteristic, you can always become what you may not be at this very moment.

Life is a gift, and it offers us the privilege, opportunity, and responsibility to give something back by becoming more.

The difference between a successful person and others is not a lack of strength, not a lack of knowledge, but rather a lack of will.

# 3

## *Prepared for the Unexpected*

I CAN BUILD YOU *a computer for that price.* This is the statement that changed everything. At the time I said it, it wasn't as simple as it feels to write today. It was loaded! It was scary, complicated, unexpected, courageous, confident and compassionate. It was destiny wrapped inside one sentence.

"I can build you a computer for that price." The weight of it marked the beginning of the rest of my life.

Thrown out of my mouth so quickly, I couldn't take it back. Once it reached the nice woman holding her coupon ad in front of me and fell on the ears of her disappointed children sitting behind her, that was it! I was fully committed to a new direction for my life.

It was 2001, I was 24 years old, a senior in college and working at Best Buy. My computer science major hadn't gotten me into any internships, so I did what I had to do to excel where I was.

I walked the aisles of Best Buy busting my behind to sell electronics and helping every customer I could reach in the store. I worked so hard that I became the store's top seller and one of the top sellers in the region within a few months.

Sure, the recognition felt great, but that feeling only lasted a few short moments. After a while, I had to take an honest look around and come to a realization — I was still broke.

*I'm constantly making money for this big corporation.* I thought to myself. *And they're not paying me any more than the next guy.* I felt stuck and underappreciated. I was bringing in the big bucks for them, while I was still struggling to pay my bills at home. Nothing about that felt right.

I made up my mind to not spend the rest of my life like this, living a paycheck-to-paycheck routine with limited advancement and no personal growth toward my calling or passions in life.

How was I going to change my situation around? I didn't know. The light bulb hadn't gone off yet. I was in the dark about the details. But, like I said, my mind was made up, and sometimes, a made-up mind is all you need to open the door to the biggest opportunities of your life.

It wasn't long before a poor family walked into the store, asked me for help and unintentionally flipped the switch to the light that I was waiting to see.

The family was looking for their first computer, but they didn't have a lot of money to spend. Even worse, the mom had failed to read the fine print of a Best Buy ad curled in her hand. She didn't realize she would have to pay the original price upfront before receiving the advertised rebate. The more I explained the details of the ad, the more the faces of the children drooped. I couldn't bare the sight of the kids sitting there sad and disappointed. It reminded me of myself growing up.

As the conversation came to a close and she turned to walk away, I jumped out of my comfort zone. Filled with passion, I yelled out, "Wait a minute, ma'am!"

She paused and turned back to face me. "Yes?" she asked.

"Listen, I can build you a computer for that price," I said, walking closer. "The same price you thought you were going to pay today." I knew I had the proper resources, skills and knowledge from my college schoolwork to help her.

"If you'd be willing to give me this opportunity," I continued, "I'd love to do this for you and your family."

"Of course," she said smiling without hesitation.

Little did she know, I was probably more excited than she was. It marked the day my light bulb lit up and never died out. It was time to get to work doing what I loved.

When your light bulb goes off, it means the ball is now in *your* court. It's *your* responsibility to make a move forward. It's not about the level of education you've achieved or the amount of support you have or don't have. Moving forward and seizing the opportunity will be *your* part!

Who cares if you hate the situation you're in! I hated my situation at Best Buy, but I was able to use it to my advantage. With everything negative comes something positive close behind. Opportunities are all around, but it's your job to see them and figure out how to get to where you want to be.

Did I know anything about building a business or writing a business plan when I first started? Not at all. I had to put in the energy and determination to find out. If you don't have the drive to keep moving up the ladder, you'll be stagnant for the rest of your life. Self-motivation can be defined as discontentment, because discontentment is the catalyst for change. Intolerance of the present creates a future.

Soon after talking with the mother of that family, I shut myself away in the back area of Best Buy's appliance department and started googling 'how to start a business' and 'how to write a business plan.' Every time I got the chance, I would sneak away to that back area and work on my plan.

The foundation of my new business was built around the idea of helping low-income families get computers. Operating as a wholesale technology distributor, I figured I could build desktop and laptop systems at prices they could afford. Even some of the largest manufacturers and retailers were ignoring them as a market, but being someone who grew up poor,

I had first-hand experience with the needs of the unfortunate.

As I explored this mission in my heart, I continued to expound on the goal of bridging the "digital divide" that separates our society's less fortunate from receiving the benefits of information technology. Regardless of background or income, everyone would get access to quality computers, as well as software, training, customized systems, repair and other services.

I told one of my best friends in college, Valdez Grant, who was also an engineer major at the time, about joining me on this idea, and he loved it. Together, mostly working out of my apartment, him and I went to work, building out the company's plan for growth and activation. We registered our company name as C&V Technologies and we quickly purchased business cards.

We were not only building desktops and laptops but also going into offices to do IT work. Most of our first clients came through me simply by reaching out to people walking the aisles of Best Buy. Whenever I'd meet someone from a low-income family looking for a better price, I would mention what I was doing on the side. I'd walk them around to the computers on display, point out their different components and then explain how I could put them all together affordably for them.

Valdez and I did such great work that clients started to spread the word. Before long, people were walking into Best Buy asking for me by name.

Given the chance to help people all while working with computers, I knew that I was slowly reaching a milestone in my life. But I had no idea that this process was preparing me for something greater than I had ever imagined.

A little over a month after starting my business, a scruffy man wearing cargo shorts, a t-shirt and flip flops walked into Best Buy near closing time. None of the other salesmen in the store wanted to work with him. "He's not about to buy anything," they whispered, judging him

based on his clothes and ungroomed appearance. I didn't agree with what they were saying,
but instead of arguing with their point of view,
I kindly walked over to the customer to talk to
him myself.

"Hi, how can I help you, sir?" I asked politely.

"I'm just looking at a few computers for my
kids. I'm thinking about buying something."

"Okay, great," I said smiling. "I'll be glad to
help you."

Over the next hour or so, I walked him
around the store and compared the features of
several computers. By the end of the night, he
came to the register with over five thousand
dollars' worth of merchandise.

"Hey, I don't know how to set this stuff up,"
he said during his checkout. "I was wondering
if you'd come and set it up for me."

"We offer a service for it," I replied. "But I
don't work in that department."

"Look, I like you. You've helped me so much. I'd like it if you would be the one making the extra money."

At this point, I couldn't refuse his offer.

"Well, I can come by when I get off."

"Great. I'll leave your name at the gate," he said, grabbed his bags and walked out of the front doors, just as scrappy and carefree as he walked in.

*The gate?* I thought to myself, rehearsing what he said. *Must be a really nice neighborhood.*

When I pulled up to the area later that night, it was way better than just a nice neighborhood. It was the Country Club.

Grinning from ear to ear, I stated my name to the security man. He nodded his head to confirm he was expecting me and raised the gate.

I was in.

His neighborhood, his home, even his driveway was gorgeous. I'd say it was one of the nicest homes I had ever seen in person. Nonetheless, I didn't try to overextend my stay. It took me 45 minutes to set up all the computers and the network.

When I was done, I wrote down my number and told him to give me a call if he had any problems. As he walked me to the door, he politely handed me a 500-dollar check. (*Yes, $500 that quickly!*)

When I got in my car, I sat there quietly thinking for about five minutes. *Did I really just get paid 500 dollars for basically an hour of work?* I thought about how many hours I would have needed to work at Best Buy to accumulate 500 dollars. The numbers were insane. Up until this point in my life, making that much money in one hour seemed unreal. This was an open door to the possibilities of my future.

My next move had to be a smart one.

The next day, I went to the bank and asked if I could open a business account with 500 dollars. Of course, I had never attempted to do anything like this and didn't know that I needed an Employer Identification Number (EIN) to open an account. They had to instruct me on how to apply for one and then welcomed me back the next day to deposit the check.

A week later, while driving, my phone rang. It was the same customer I set up computers for that night.

"I was very impressed by your work," he said. "How do you feel about a career change?"

"I have a degree in computer science," I responded quickly. "I'm always looking to advance myself."

"Great," he said. "Come to my office tomorrow morning at 8:30 AM."

***

Things were moving fast. I showed up promptly the next morning, anticipating where this opportunity was going to take me. You know, it's one thing to have an idea, but it's another thing to bring that idea to life. Most run into problems when they try to figure out how to create their dream but fail to realize that this phase starts with a conversation or an experience.

"Where do you see yourself in the next five to seven years?" he asked, opening the interview. He was the Executive Vice President of a Fortune 500 company.

"That's a great question," I said, pausing for a moment. "Well, if I'm able to start working here, I know I'll be able to move up because I am a self-motivated individual. I'm very smart and I learn fast. I think I'll do well here. But, if I'm not, I planned on doing what I did for you for others. I've looked into starting my own business doing computer services."

"Really?" he asked in a surprised tone. "Elaborate."

I told him about the poor family I helped a few weeks before he walked into the store. In the middle of finishing the story, he stops me.

"Hold on," he said, reaching for his phone.

He calls a friend — Charles D'Agostino, who happened to be the CEO of the largest incubator in the state of Louisiana and also had the number one small business incubator program in the nation at the time.

"Hey," he said to the guy on the other end of phone. "I have a young man in my office. He's smart and intuitive. He wants to start a business, and I know you guys help entrepreneurs and all. I want to send him over to you. Let him hear what you have to say and we'll talk later."

When he got off the phone, he wrote down Charles contact information and handed it to me.

"Go see him tomorrow," he said. "See what he has to say. If you like it, go for it. If you feel like it's not what you want to do and it's not your true path, come back and see me. We'll look at putting you in a position here. Let's see if we can make your dream a reality."

Just like that, my life altered again. I was headed down an unknown path of even more opportunities. The next morning, I sat down with the Charles and listened to what he had to say. We ended up talking for a very long time. During the interview, he realized I had a great idea up my sleeve and showed interest in moving forward with me.

"Okay, then," he said, wrapping up. "Have you started on a business plan?"

"Yes!" I blurted out. "I actually have one."

I was so excited to be prepared for this question. I thought my business plan was well written and organized.

Well, that's what I thought until I turned it over to him and his team. I received it back with red marks covering every sentence and section. *Whoa!* I laughed to myself. *Looked like I turned in a bad essay paper to a teacher.*

"Make the changes," he said. "When you finish, come back and see us, and we'll go from there."

In four days, I showed up with the business plan totally revised.

*Four days!* I wasn't playing around.

When I walked in, they were expecting me to have more questions and not the entire plan revamped.

"I'm done!" I said smiling.

"You're finished?" he asked, making sure he heard what I said correctly.

"Yes, I'm done. I've added all the things you've asked me to."

I shocked both him and his team. They never had someone *this* passionate about getting started. You see, I recognized the meeting was only the first step; I knew a forcible next step would have to follow if I was going to succeed here.

I jumped in running. I ran so fast that two years after turning in my business plan, I became the company's Client of the Year.

Sounds great, right? It was. But could I quit my day job and be an entrepreneur full-time?

Not yet.

I figured out how to keep the dream alive. Part-time.

# Leadership:

*The ability to follow is the first qualification for leadership.*

Do you see anyone around that you admire? Pay attention. Ask questions. Appreciate their advice. Watch how they carry themselves, how they shake hands and they maneuver through crowds and interact with others.

Instead of opening your mouth before your time, spend time standing back and paying attention. It will help you become the person you want to be. When you're observant with hopes of learning to become better at something, you'll be following that person's lead and quietly developing yourself.

When you finally step out on your own (as a leader), people will start to follow *you*. And even then, as a leader, you'll still find someone else you can learn from. The cycle of following and leading (learning and teaching) never stops.

Often what may appear as a detour in life is actually the most direct and empowering path to your destination.

The real world does not reward perfectionists. It rewards people who get things done.

# 4

## *Dreaming Despite All Odds*

FOCUS ON YOUR dreams. But don't neglect the uncomfortable things that have to be done to reach them. You may not want to work a day job while hustling to build your own business, but if the circumstance calls for it, find some satisfaction in landing a position that will support your entrepreneurial dreams in the long run.

This is why I left Best Buy and started as a sales manager in the computer department of CompUSA. If you've ever visited a CompUSA store, you know that in comparison to Best Buy, it's more of a technology store. Best Buy mainly focuses on electronics.

At CompUSA, I was able to sharpen my skills, study the field and even read a few of their books in the computer department. I would often take the opportunity to visit their technology lab and ask questions such as: *What's wrong with this computer? What are you guys working on? What's the solution to fixing this?* I figured things out quickly and taught myself how to actually do what I had only observed or read about.

Having a day job — the right kind of job in your field — can pay off if it adds to your dreams instead of takes away from it. In college, we learned how to program computers, not how to build them, so the CompUSA job was great for teaching me more about the building process. Plus, it was fun to continue capitalizing on my skills in sales.

Upper management had taken notice of my work ethic and frequently expressed how impressed they were. However, not everyone on the management team thought I was fit for the job.

The general manager, in particular, didn't want me to move up. When the district team looked into promoting me to store manager, he found a way to fire me.

"You just let an educated man go," I said on my way out the door. "I appreciate it. Have a good life."

For four months, I went without work. I lived off of a $250 unemployment check until I found an open position at Office Depot. For a year, I worked there as an operations manager. Then, one day, the man who managed me at Best Buy came into the store and offered to recruit me to work for Kirschman's, a furniture store he was now running.

I had never sold furniture in my life, and honestly, I didn't want to. But he was offering more money so I made the move.

As I stated earlier, it's best to find a position that supports your entrepreneurial dreams. At Kirschman's, I felt as if I wasn't fulfilling what I set out to do. I was unhappy. I remember taking off a few days to go on a trip with my best friends, and when I came home, I thought to myself, *If they tell me one thing I don't like today, I'm quitting!*

Low and behold, when I walked in the next day, they said they weren't happy with me taking weekends off and that they were no longer allowing it.

*That's my cue*, I thought.

"Thank you for the opportunity," I said. "Today is my last day."

I shook their hands and walked out. I never looked back at that store — or any store, for that matter. I sat in my car and told God I was going to trust Him moving forward.

I didn't look for another job. I stepped out in faith and went full-time and full-energy into entrepreneurship. At an early age, I understood that I was the secret to my own success. But now, it was more serious than just understanding it. I had to realize the raw truth behind being the secret to my own success every morning.

Thanks to my mentor meetings with Charles, I was able to hone in on my skill set. Although my education was in computer science, my real skill was (and still is) my mouthpiece. People are doing business with "the person" over the product, and so my personality held the key to the growth of my business. I've learned that you can have the best product in the industry, but people will rather go where they get the best customer service. I also learned to pay close attention to my customers. Customers will always tell you what direction you should in.

Continuing to meet with Charles, I better understood the customer and the market and what it took to be successful, long-term. There were so many things Valdez and I weren't doing just because we didn't know they existed. We had a lot to learn about running a business.

The Two D's of Development:

Determination - a firm or fixed intention to achieve a desired end.

Discipline - training that corrects, molds or perfects mental faculties and moral character.

Every day, you wake up to a new beginning. God has given you that blessing. Take it. *Allow* yourself to be successful with every new start.

# 5

## *A Gift in Action*

E VERY MORNING, I looked in the mirror and said, "You will be successful today, tomorrow, this week, this month, this year — no matter what anyone says. I believe in you." It was a small but important adjustment.

Believing in yourself is the first step to becoming a successful entrepreneur and an overall successful person. There's no way to be successful if you don't first believe in yourself. Throughout my life, I've met extremely talented people in various industries, and all of those who were successful had one thing in common: confidence.

Someone once told me that you can be the smartest person with the greatest invention, but if you have no confidence or drive, you will never succeed. This goes to prove that what you believe you see when you look in the mirror will be the determining factor of your success.

Try doing something I did for years. Stand in front of the mirror and say, *Today, I make a stand and a promise to forever believe in myself. I will only surround myself with positive energy and positive people. If I don't believe in myself, no one else will.*

In the mirror, see a person who has aspirations and goals and the ability to get it all done. It's up to you to take this first step elevating your life and business.

When you've stepped out on your own, totally believing in yourself and your mission, what happens next? You accept your gifts, talents and purposes and put them to work with confidence. What you're here on earth to do has ever-increasing potential, and once you recognize this, your great business idea will be just as limitless.

Every business starts with a great idea. To avoid losing momentum on your path to bringing it to life, try writing it down in a notebook. On the front of the notebook, label it "The Great Idea."

Whatever your idea is, trust me, it'll always point back to your gifts. Maybe you're great with talking to people, or cooking, or working with electronics, or sewing. There is no limit to what you are capable of achieving once you believe in yourself and identify your gifts and purpose for those gifts.

\*\*\*

Things were going great. For two months, as a full-time entrepreneur, it was great.

After two months, Hurricane Katrina hit the Gulf Coast. Two months of good work, and then one of the deadliest hurricanes in the history of the United States made landfall in Southeast Louisiana, causing over fifty breaches in New Orleans' surge protection. In two months, my city was completely under water and my promising future as a new entrepreneur didn't look so promising.

Carrying around a dream that was still alive in the middle of the chaos, I searched for ways to inject my gift into places where people needed it most. *Isn't this what our gifts are made for?* It's what our purposes live for. They only exist to bring life to others, especially in times of devastation.

The first opportunity I had to give came through the Louisiana Legislative Black Caucus. My team helped set up computers for their emergency call center. When the job was done, I continued to attend the caucus weekly updates, as I was looking for more ways to help.

One of the members who knew what my intentions were had advised me to become a vendor for the Federal Emergency Management Agency (FEMA).

Immediately, I went on the Internet and researched 'how to do business with the federal government.' Once I learned the process for working with FEMA, I signed up as an emergency responder, listed my firm's inventory and abilities, and I waited to see what would happen next.

***

Valdez and I were working around the clock to deliver products from our "headquarters," which happened to still be my two-bedroom apartment. Valdez had also recently gotten accepted into a PhD program at Purdue University in Indiana. He was going to be leaving to pursue a different path, but he expressed that he wanted me to continue doing my thing with the business. The beauty in this was that he didn't hold me back and I didn't hold him back.

During this time, in addition to limited space and computer inventory covering the floors, I had twelve evacuated family members living with me, including my mother.

One early morning, around 7 o'clock, my mom burst through my bedroom door, pressing the phone against her chest.

"FEMA's on the phone," she whispered.

"Huh?" I squinted, slowly leaning forward to hear her better.

"FEMA!" She whispered as loudly as she possibly could without being heard over the phone.

Realizing what she said, I jumped up, reached out my hand for the phone and cleared my throat.

"Yes, this is Calvin," I answered, hand-motioning my mom to leave the room and close the door.

"We got your number from the local vendor list," the guy said on the other end. "Were you affected by the hurricane?"

"I wasn't," I said thankfully.

They were looking for a minority tech business to help with rebuilding and my company was the only one listed. *Can you believe that?*

"Can you supply 300 laptops?" he asked.

I paused. Supplying 300 laptops was way out of my league. I asked him to give me a couple of hours to make some calls and get the quantity together.

Unfortunately, with the time frame given, I came up short. I missed out on that contract, but I didn't miss out on the opportunity to help FEMA in other ways.

When the second contract came around, I was ready. After fulfilling a contract worth $2,500, I had my foot in the door.

I was excited! Ecstatic, even. In fact, I wanted to personally thank the contracting officer.

So, that's exactly what I did.

I had no idea it would be another life-altering decision. Who knew so much more could be waiting around the corner of a genuine *thank you*? This one 'thank you' brought my business to extraordinary levels.

How extraordinary exactly? Well, I'll get into that in the next chapter.

# Patience:

### *Patience is the weapon that forces deception to reveal itself.*

We live in a time where instant gratification reigns. As a result, people like to rush into things. But, when someone rushes, they don't pay attention to what's around them. They get fooled and don't realize when they are seeing deception.

When you are going through life as an entrepreneur, you can want growth and the freedom to do what you want so badly that you rush into it without paying attention to your surroundings. I remember being so excited to get started that I skipped over the important stuff — like making sure my taxes were done correctly and I had the right accounts. At the time, all I wanted was money and to be my own boss, but it required so much more of me.

At the end of the day, it is best to take your time, pay attention to where you are when you start and be patient in the process of growth. Don't be so quick to make a move, because you can unnecessarily mess things up for yourself. If you're patient, it is more likely that you will see what you're supposed to see to make the best possible move or decision.

Your attitude determines the season you enter.

Less gossiping, more learning. Less complaining, more excelling. Less walls, more bridges. Less fear, more courage.

# 6

## *The Power of Thank You*

I GOT UP.

I got dressed.

I drove down to the local FEMA office.

Parked my car and took a moment to gather my thoughts. I picked up my phone and dialed the number of the contracting officer.

*Was I doing too much by calling?*

The contracting officer had never met me and never asked to. Her job was to sign me up to fulfill the contract and then to receive the work. That's it. That was all it was ever supposed to be.

Except, being the enthusiastic go-getter that I was (and *still* am) behind my passions, I had to go the extra mile. I had to do more. I just *had* to say, "Thank you."

If I have a good feeling about doing something — even if it's totally off the charts, I do it. Doing it is a part of who I am. It's about going all in and not holding back an ounce of effort. Remember what I mentioned in the first chapter? When I see something I want in life, I go for it. My mom taught me that. And sometimes going for it means turning back to show gratitude and appreciation for even the smallest opportunities.

I never did anything like this before — driving to a place just to say thank you in person. But I knew this first contract job with the government was a great start for where I wanted to be, and I was grateful for the person who decided to trust my new company to handle the work.

"This is Calvin Mills," I said to the lady who picked up. "I'm the gentlemen with CMC Technology Solutions. I wanted to say thank you for giving me the opportunity to fulfill the last contract. I'm actually here and I want to meet you face to face. I want you to be able to put a face with the name." (*By this time, Valdez had moved away and the company name was changed to CMC [Calvin Mills Consulting] Technology Solutions.*)

"Okay, definitely," she said. "I'll be right out."

She came out to meet me in the parking lot. After shaking hands, she asked if I had some time to come inside.

With the havoc of Hurricane Katrina, things were hectic inside of FEMA's office. Phones were ringing off the hook. Mountains of thick folders covered every desk. Tense conversations filled the space. It was hard to hear myself think. Everyone was running around trying to get things done.

Through the turbulence, we made it to her private office and shut the door. It was calmer inside, but the three-feet high stack of papers were screaming just as loud.

"Can you *please* go through this?" she asked, slightly tilting her head in the direction of the outrageous stack, hoping I had come to rescue her.

Technically, I had.

It was meant to be, if you ask me. What were the odds of me spontaneously showing up at the office on a day she needed me the most?

"I don't mind at all," I said, staring at the mountain of opportunities.

"Thank you!" she yelled out, relieved. "Tell me if you find anything you can do for us in this stack. I'll confirm it and authorize it right away. Oh, and how do you want to get paid? We can do Net 30 or a credit card payment?"

*Is this really happening?* I stretched my eyes. It all seemed too good to be true. But it was definitely ALL true and all happening!

"Credit card is fine," I answered with confidence, knowing I didn't even have a credit card merchant account set up yet. I didn't let that worry me, because at that very moment, my company had reached its greatest turning point.

All because I decided to get up and say thank you. Two words. That's all it took.

This moment ultimately led to our company winning a total of $350,000 in contracts over the next few months, supplying computers for FEMA, schools and offices in the affected areas. In less than three months, I went from a $2,500 contract to obtaining $350,000 worth of contract work.

Let me point this out. Persistence changes things, as well sacrifice, self-motivation and gratitude. It all matters because it all attracts the elevation and momentum you're looking to achieve as an entrepreneur. Nothing surpasses your level of consistency and gratefulness. Trust me. It's been proven time and time again through my journey.

The contracting officer I met that day nominated me for the Department of Homeland Security Small Business Outstanding Performance Award.

I won it.

It blew me away. It still amazes me when I think about it today.

It was the very first time I'd been recognized as a small business owner, and to have the recognition come from the federal government was a big deal!

Soon after, we landed a small business loan of $20,000 and then amazed the loan officer by repaying it in four days. Our network grew over the next several years, as we were hired by universities and colleges to set up wireless networks on their campuses. We even worked with mega corporations like Walmart and Hewlett-Packard.

But the ups of success do not come without the downs. It's about not getting caught up in the ups or the downs. I want you to understand that even when it's bad, it's still good. It's all about how you respond to the situation in front of you. And until you get to a point where you can truly hone in on those skills of responding properly, you'll never get it!

Many times, when entrepreneurs and business owners first start their companies, they get extremely excited. They see who they can be in the future if everything goes as they've always dreamed. At the same time, most are scared and confused and don't have a lot of information or experience. What's missing from majority of their lives are two things: confidence and faith.

If you want to be an entrepreneur, at some point you will have to step out on faith and just go for it. If you never go for it, you'll never know if it can be successful. Take a look at all the successful people you know or admire. The one thing they all will have in common is that they stepped out and took a chance.

Everybody has a great idea, but who's willing to step out and take a chance on it? It's comfortable to fill out an application, go through an interview and get hired. Sure, you can say "Oh, I'll have a definite check on the 1st and the 15th. So, I'm safe." But it takes a special person to step out and say, "I have no clue when I am going to get paid, but I know what I can control. That's getting up every day, going for it, and making an opportunity for myself." That's the key.

You have to step out and trust your skill set and trust your idea, but not only that — you have to work! And a lot of people aren't willing to do that. They rather clock-in for eight hours, not do much of anything, and settle for a comfortable check twice a month. If a growing entrepreneur sat back and didn't do much of anything, they could be starving. There's no room to be comfortable in entrepreneurship. Going for it with confidence and faith is the only way through.

Will you fail? That's up to you. I've never accepted failure. Even when the things I cherished most were stripped away from me. I still didn't accept it. The difference between average people and successful people is their perception of failure and response to failure.

What you have to realize for yourself is that there is no failure — there are only lessons learned. I wouldn't say I've failed at anything. I may not have done some things right, but I didn't fail. I learned a lesson and moved forward.

# Humility:

*Those in high places can be brought down. Those in low places can be called up. Humility is the awareness of it.*

As fast as you can get success is as fast as it can go away. The one thing I realized through my journey is that my success didn't happen by accident. It came through people who were connected to me and all the things I was surrounded by. It was like I had been positioned my entire life to reach success, and because I recognized how success came through my connection to others, I never got arrogant or thought I was better than someone else.

There was one young man I mentored years ago who had a taste of success and immediately afterward became very prideful about it. He lost focus. When you think fame and recognition means that you've made it, you'll fail every time. That should never be what you're focused on.

There are two primary choices in life: to accept conditions as they are, or accept the responsibility for changing them.
You choose.

The size of your success is measured by three things:
the strength of your desire, the size of your dream, and how you handle disappointment along the way.

# 7

## *All Roads Lead to Destiny*

I'VE BEEN JOBLESS, living on unemployment benefits. I've dealt with clients who disappeared without paying. I've dealt with business challenges that felt unbearable, but the most detrimental experience of all was having to still thrive in business while going through a divorce.

My normal way of living abruptly pivoted when my ex-wife and I separated. It totally caught me off guard. I had to deal with this during the time of the recession. Client calls were slow and business was at an all-time low when I was forced to leave my home and live in my office.

By this time, my company had an *actual* office (an upgrade from my two-bedroom apartment from years before). I had about five people working with me and none them had a clue that I was sleeping there at night. I never said anything. I slept on an air mattress, with no TV, no hot water — nothing. All the luxuries I was used to were gone. Times were so scarce and depressing that I considered going back into corporate America as a way to survive it. I even wrestled with the thought that maybe entrepreneurship wasn't for me.

I felt confused, angry and low. But I wasn't looking for anyone to feel sorry for me. I also didn't take the energy to feel sorry for myself, because in turn, that would've been a loss of precious time on actually building myself. Looking back, I see that it was the best thing for me at the time. I had no distractions, and for the first time *ever*, I became an avid reader. A lot of what I learned in those books helped me get through this time stronger. It guided me in re-evaluating my life.

An unforgettable turning point happened one night as I was turning up my office heater to withstand the unbearable cold shower I was about to take. Something clicked. I started laughing, hysterically. *I get it.* I said to myself. I knew what was going on. It wasn't my job to do God's job in my life. I had to give it to Him, completely. "You're in control," I said to God. "I'm only going to do what I'm supposed to do." When I woke up the next day, I felt different.

That morning I got a call from Valdez. Him and another friend of mine had bought me a plane ticket to visit him in Dallas for a few days. They knew what I was dealing with and insisted on me getting away for a while.

He was right. I needed to get away. So, I packed and headed for Dallas. My time hanging out there was amazing. I was in such a better place mentally. I had already decided not to give up. The night before I chose to dig deep and move in faith, as I had during the beginning stages of building my business. And here's what is so great about making your mind up to press through: you set yourself to win!

When I got back in town from Dallas, text messages and phone calls immediately started pouring in with new business opportunities. With one powerful thought in the right direction, I was able to refocus and regain my steps toward what I was called to do. I had been living in my office for almost seven months, but things started to quickly make a turn for the best.

Motivation comes from within and things can change at any moment in your favor. If you are not happy with where you are, realize that it's only temporary. *Really* see it as temporary! When I was unhappy, I still smiled because I knew it wasn't my end point. It was only a temporary place to get me to my next step and to where I truly wanted to be in the long run. My goal has always been set on being a difference maker, a leader.

Face unhappiness and disappointment by preparing an exit plan — a plan for how you will walk away from the situation. If you want something different, you must figure out what has to be done to get there. If you don't do this, you'll continue to be stagnant and unhappy.

Having preparation, focus and determination is such a big deal! It's big in every aspect. The three go together so well that I wish I could make them one word: *preparationfocusdetermination*. That's how strongly I feel about it.

My preparationfocusdetermination walked me into my destiny. If you're not focused on what you want and determined to make it happen, it doesn't matter how great your idea is on paper or in your mind. It'll never come to life.

When new opportunities were presented to me, I jumped on them. Likewise, you have to operate in the same tenacity. Don't lag. Motivate yourself every day. I was constantly motivated growing up, and I'm just as motivated today.

You see, many times I find individuals say, "Oh, that's impossible to do." But, for me, as a God-fearing person, I look at the word 'impossible' and see 'I'm possible' every time. I believe God is really telling us that *we are* possible.

Whether it was being told I was wasting my time playing football and later winning three championships and having the chance to play in the NFL or losing my job and being broke and then gaining success with my own businesses — I've always believed anything is possible.

Taking negativity and turning it into something positive has been my stance through the process. I used the hurtful situations to fuel what I wanted to do and get me to where I am today. It has also allowed me to motivate others. Those who've seen the things I've gone through or heard the story of my journey often say, "If you can do it, I know it can be possible for me."

I wasn't born with a silver spoon in my mouth. I was born with a plastic spoon, and I took that plastic spoon and gold plated it through hard work and persistence.

I want you to take a really good look at my story. I came from a poor environment, single-parent home, victim of bullying, not considered the smartest kid in the classroom and became successful in both life and business. Take a look at my story and say, "Okay, I can become whatever I set my mind to accomplish."

Your big opportunity to make it out of your situation doesn't have to come from a sports league or famous recognition in entertainment. You can create your own impact, wealth and legendary path in your own lane as an entrepreneur.

Through the years, I went from being known as just Calvin Mills to Calvin the Football Player to Calvin the Computer Guy to Mr. Mills, the CEO. I've been in business since 2002, and I've managed to grow it year after year. When you put the work in, people recognize it and respect the place you've earned and created. You gain the platform you need to be a true, difference-making leader.

Today, I'm in my early 40s and have already accomplished so much in my life. I am the father of four amazing children (one boy, two girls and one step daughter), happily married to my beautiful wife and an award-winning serial entrepreneur. I've been featured in major business publications, named the face of Louisiana for entrepreneurship, a philanthropist and motivational speaker. I've received national recognition and the backing of global companies. I've been awarded placement as one of the Top 50 Businesses invited to the White House, and most recently, I was honored by Southern University and the city of Baton Rouge.

As far as the money I've curated over the years, let's just say I'm thousands of times better off than I was as a kid, and I've fulfilled my promise to take care of my mom.

If you trust in the power of God, every good thing you ask for will come to fruition. Don't accept where you currently are as the end result for your life; it's all temporary. Every situation you go through is a road leading you into a greater place found in your destiny. You have to know it and persistently pursue it.

# Commitment:

*Commitment is your final decision to meet the needs of the ones you were called to serve.*

Through my journey, I stayed true to what I believed in, despite when contracts stopped and business got quiet. I continued to believe in what I had started from the beginning and what I was on the cusp of achieving.

I was committed to watching my dreams come to life. I know entrepreneurs can get discouraged and second-guess their purpose when things don't turn out the way they imagined, but the ones who push past that time will always come out on top. The ones who stay committed to their overall idea and their overall passion find success.

Commitment and faith goes together. If you believe in what you're doing and see it for yourself, don't give up.

Do not dwell in the past.
Do not get lost in the
dreams of the future.
Rather, concentrate your
thoughts on the present
moment.

When you listen, it's amazing what you can learn. When you act on what you've learned, it's amazing what you can change.

# Interview

## AN ENTREPRENEUR

*Have a closer look into my journey.*

## What habits contribute to your success?

*When I think about what allowed me to be where I am today, it's definitely my loyalty and determination factor. I've always had the habit of being loyal to the direction I wanted to go and what I wanted to do. Without wandering into a different lane, I stayed determined in the path set before me. I understood early on that I couldn't just sit down and expect things to fall on my lap, but I had to be a go-getter. I had to do the research, find out how to start the business, how to make the connection, how to write the plan, etc.*

*In addition, I've learned to listen before I talk and to receive criticism without feeling offended. And I must say, football has helped me build the habit of practice. I quickly put all the skills I learn into practice in hopes of winning in every circumstance I face.*

## How did you learn from failure?

*Being told "no" over and over, being poor growing up, being bullied and being labeled as the "different" one who doesn't fit in has toughened my skin. By the time I hit college, I knew that failing at something didn't mean it was over for me. I adapted to what I failed at, so when it was time to try it again, I didn't repeat the same mistakes. I'd try something new. The more I failed and tried again at the same situations, the more I learned, adapted and conquered the failing problems at hand. I continued to move forward — just with a different step the next time.*

## What are your suggestions for new startups?

*Make sure you have an overall focus on exactly what it is that you want to do, and then take your time and be patient. It's not going to happen overnight. You have to be patient with your company. Be able to accept criticism and don't be afraid to ask for help from individuals who are in the same industry as you.*

## How did you make your first sale?

*My first sale came from the desire to help a family that was in need. Because I was willing and able to show them a different route to get a better outcome, it turned into a sale.*

## How did you develop key partnerships?

*Well, I took it upon myself to introduce myself to the people I wanted to partner with. I looked at their strengths and weaknesses, and I saw how they can help me and how I can help them. When it was time to approach them, I introduced myself and what I knew they needed. I'd ask for an opportunity to help them. It's always an "opportunity" for you to help, never a service or product you're desperate to sell. Mentioning how I could help them would open doors left and right for me.*

*Another aspect I'd like to point out is the power of simply asking. Sometimes all you have to do is ask. You'll be surprised by the outcomes it can produce.*

## How can you minimize the unknowns in building a business?

*Honestly, you can't. It's unknown, right? You can't predict it or see it coming. All you can do is prepare yourself as best as possible. Preparation will at least minimize the damage. Sure, some situations will hit you out of nowhere, but if you are prepared for things that can potentially happen, you'll be able to handle yourself better than if you weren't prepared at all. For instance, let's say you're hit with a financial setback. If you've prepared for potential financial downturns, you'll be able to minimize the damage before it happens.*

*So, how can you best prepare for what you can't see coming? Prepare for any and all possible situations you can think of.*

**How did you distinguish yourself from your competitors?**

*Distinguishing myself happened organically. I truly believe that I offer what no one else does. There are individuals and businesses that fix computers, provide tech support and equipment but rarely do you find a company that does it all! Plus, my personality alone sets me apart. The relationships I've built have come from the strength of my personality. I've never done an advertisement campaign. It's been strictly word of mouth — which says a lot about the quality of work I offer. The main product I'm giving is really me. I'm the product. At the end of the day, I'm the distinguishing factor.*

## What was your biggest mistake?

*Getting excited too fast! I think the success I got early on caused me to get overexcited. In fact, it cost me a lot of money. After coming up as a poor kid, earning six figures was unheard of. I saw hundreds of thousands of dollars in my account and knew I could buy anything I wanted, so I splurged. Mentally, I was not prepared to receive that money. I spent without thinking and without planning for the future.*

## What would you have done differently?

*If I could go back, I probably would slow down and ask for help when I noticed things were getting to be too fast for me to handle alone. I would've especially asked for more help with my finances.*

**How do you decrease the friction that comes along with first-time customers?**

*Don't trust them so easily in the beginning. I'll explain what I mean by that. During the beginning stages of growing my business, I started to offer some clients service on credit. I would even give away my work for free. But, in doing this, people started to take advantage of me and stopped respecting me as a small business owner. And their perspective of me was all my fault!*

*It's because I gave too much trust early on and wasn't forceful enough. Of course, when trying to grow business, you want to be more lenient to please your customers, but this can backfire. I learned that it's best to think like a big company even as a small business. If I would've been less easygoing in the beginning, I could have reduced the friction created when talking about pricing or payments with clients.*

**Any tips for hiring your first employee?**

*Yes, yes! Be very selective with the person that you hire first. Definitely try to find someone who isn't exactly like you in their skills but who share some of your same characteristics. When you can trust someone's character, you can trust delegating more work to him or her while you focus on building the business. You want someone you can trust to handle those things.*

**What are you reading? Do you have any book suggestions?**

*"No Secrets to Elevation!" Besides this book, I would say dive into the many books written by David Bach. He's a financial guru. His books have helped me better understand and appreciate handling my finances as a whole, not just for business.*

**How do you keep your focus on the big picture when you're constantly faced with short-term problems and possible extermination of your startup?**

*It takes a lot of practice and a lot of faith! You must have an extreme amount of confidence that you're going in the right direction and making the right decisions. Sometimes, we are so focused on short-term matters that we hinder our long-term progress. When all you see is what's right in front of you, you lose focus of the future.*

*Let's say your numbers state you're at $1,000 in revenue today, but you want to be at $10,000 by the end of the year. In order to start multiplying your revenue today, you can't lose focus of the end goal. Seeing the long-term picture allows you to stay committed to the short-term task list. It all plays together. Begin to see how they work together, and you'll be able to avoid extermination.*

**What's your best advice for someone who has an idea but doesn't know where to start?**

*If you have an idea, here's the first thing you should do. Grab a notebook. Start writing every idea you have down. Once you have about 5-10 ideas that you like, begin researching the industries they fall into. You want to see what's already out there, see how you can do it better, or discover how you can fill in a gap. Remember, the idea doesn't have to be new, but it has to be better. I suggest finding great mentors in the field you're trying to get into. Be humble and really listen to what mentors have to say.*

*Putting your idea into action may also require that you do free labor to get the experience. Sometimes, you may even need to get a job in that field just to see how things work behind the scenes. Bringing new ideas to life takes a lot of persistence, as well as preparation, focus and determination. Be relentless about staying the course, and you'll reach every goal you set.*

Your past has determined where you are at this moment. What you do today will determine where you are tomorrow.

Now
go be
successful!

# ABOUT THE AUTHOR

Calvin Mills Jr. is an award-winning serial entrepreneur who built his platform in the information technology arena from humble beginnings. He is a former professional football player as well as a graduate of Southern University. Succeeding as the Founder, CEO and President of CMC Technology Solutions, Calvin has been featured in Entrepreneur, Fast Company, and InfoWorld publications.

From the start of his career, he has focused his pursuit on making a people-focused mark in his industry. Today, as a dynamic speaker, mentor and author, he continues to make a great difference in the lives of the next generation of entrepreneurs. He and his wife and children live in Baton Rouge, Louisiana.

## Calvin Mills, Jr.
# Honors & Awards

2017– Excellence in Leadership (Southern University & A&M College Alumni Federation)

2016 – 1 of 50 business leaders invited to the White House

2008 – Resolution from Board of Supervisors of the Southern University and A&M College System as Outstanding Alumnus

2008 – Louisiana Economic Development (LED) and U.S. Small Business Administration (SBA), Louisiana Minority Small Business Champion of the Year. (This award highlights "outstanding contributions made by Louisiana small businesses and honors excellence in entrepreneurship.")

2008 – Louisiana Economic Development (LED) and U.S. Small Business Administration (SBA), Louisiana District/Capital Region Small Business Champion of the Year

2008 and 2006 – Small Business Development Center Client of the Year, Louisiana Business & Technology Center; ranked nationally as the #1 Small Business Incubator (LSU/E.J. Ourso College of Business)

2007 – Official Statement of Recognition of

2007 – Concurrent Resolution from Louisiana State Legislature for Outstanding Achievement

2007 – City of Baton Rouge, Outstanding Business Entrepreneur

2006 – Homeland Security Award from Governor Kathleen Blanco

2006 – U.S. Department of Homeland Security, Small Business Achievement Award for Outstanding Performance

2006 and 2007 – *Madison's Who's Who of Top Executives*

95626019R00071

Made in the USA
Middletown, DE
26 October 2018